THE GREAT BOOK OF ANIMAL KNOWLEDGE

JAGUAR

Subtitle

Introduction

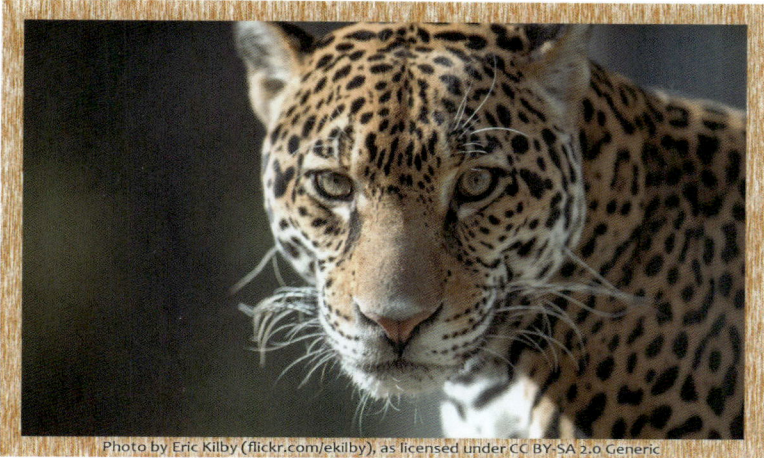

Photo by Eric Kilby (flickr.com/ekilby), as licensed under CC BY-SA 2.0 Generic

Stalking deep in the forest of the Amazon is the real king of the jungle. Armed with its incredible eyesight, camouflage fur, and extremely powerful jaws, the jaguar stalks its prey, waiting for the perfect moment. Then when the moment arrives, the jaguar leaps! It lands its teeth on the skull of its prey and kills it immediately. Jaguars are incredible hunters. They are at the top of the Amazonian food chain. Let's learn more about these amazing animals!

What Jaguars Look Like

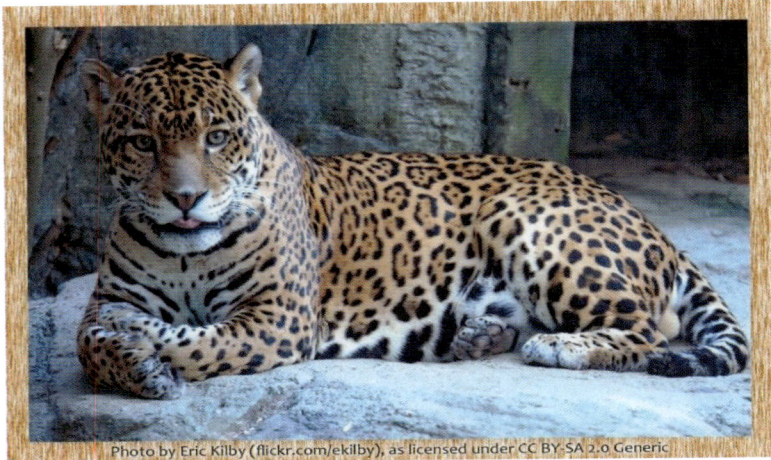

Photo by Eric Kilby (flickr.com/ekilby), as licensed under CC BY-SA 2.0 Generic

Jaguars are very fierce looking but beautiful animals. Lots of people confuse jaguars for leopards, because the two species look alike. There are a few differences though. Jaguars' bodies are stockier, they have shorter tails, and their spots are slightly different from a leopard's spots.

Size and Weight

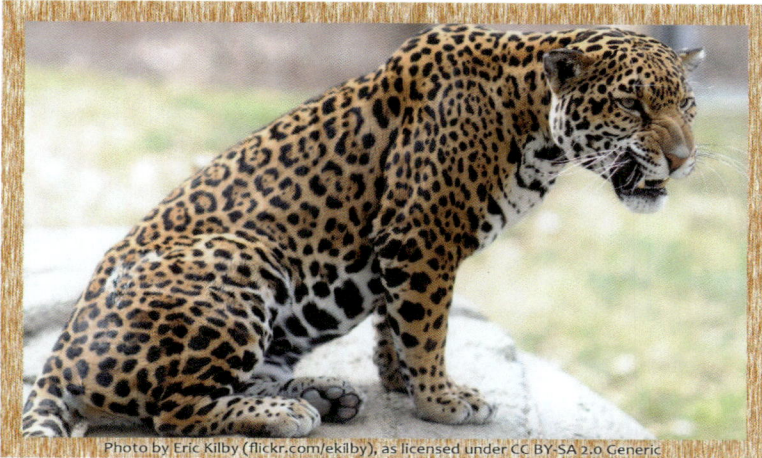

Jaguars are the largest cat found in the Americas. They are the third largest cat in the world, smaller than only lions and tigers. They can grow over 7 ft (2.1 m) from head to tail! Jaguars weigh around 100-250 pounds (45-113 kg).

Rosettes

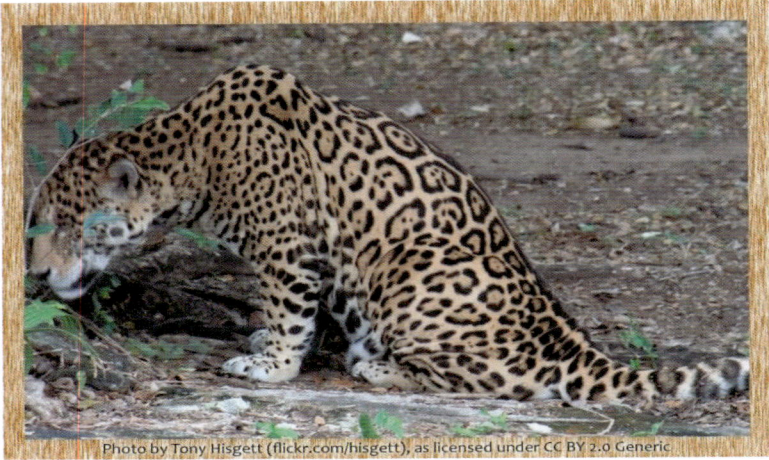

The fur of a jaguar is covered with rosettes, black spots that resemble roses. Each jaguar has a unique rosette pattern on their fur. Like human fingerprints, no two jaguars have the same coat pattern! Their yellow fur and rosettes actually provide very good camouflage in the forest, perfect for ambushing prey. Jaguars have spots in the middle of their rosettes, while leopards do not. This is one way to tell the two species apart.

Where Jaguars Live

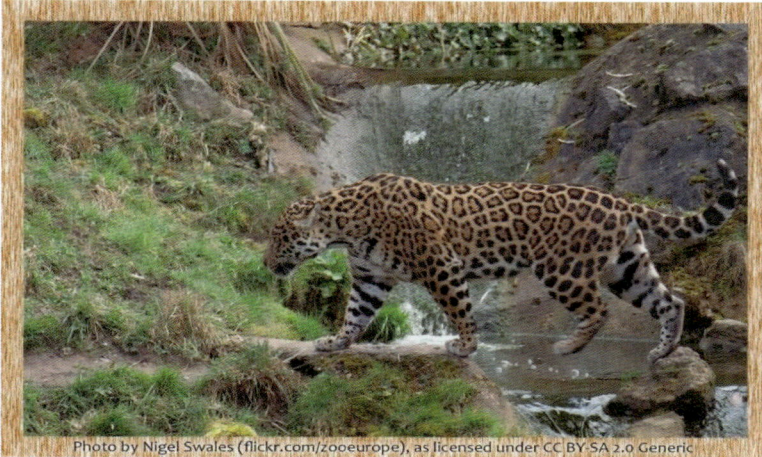

Photo by Nigel Swales (flickr.com/zooeurope), as licensed under CC BY-SA 2.0 Generic

Jaguars are the only member of the big cats found in the Americas, from Mexico to Argentina. Most of them are found on the Amazon basin. They live in rainforests, swamplands, savannas, and sometimes even deserts. They prefer living close to a body of water.

Climbing

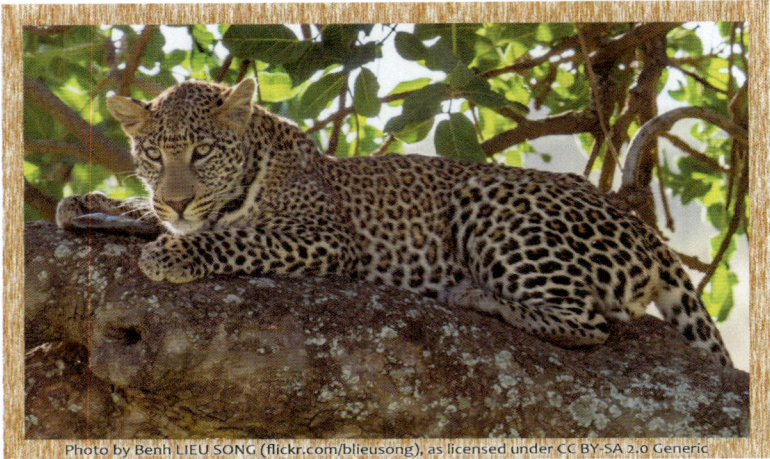

Photo by Benh LIEU SONG (flickr.com/blieusong), as licensed under CC BY-SA 2.0 Generic

Jaguars are very strong animals and they are very good at climbing trees. However, because they are the most powerful predator in their habitat, jaguars don't really have to climb trees to escape from danger and don't spend a lot of time in trees. But they do climb trees, and sometimes they ambush their prey from above.

Swimming

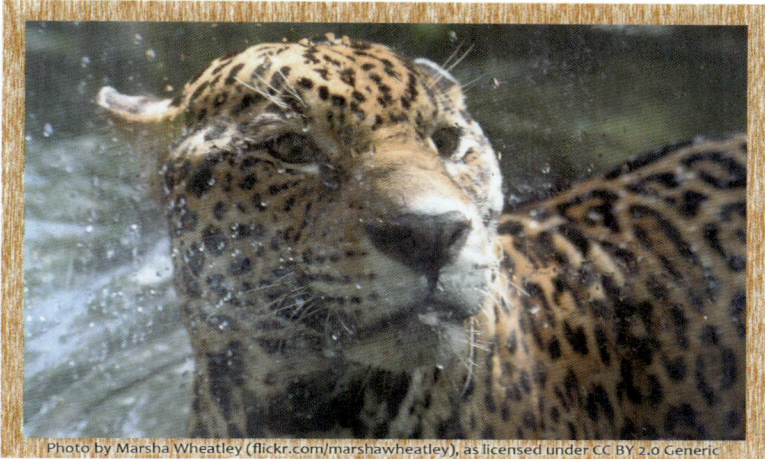

Photo by Marsha Wheatley (flickr.com/marshawheatley), as licensed under CC BY 2.0 Generic

Jaguars are very good swimmers. They rarely go far away from a river or lake. They can also hunt in the water. Jaguars can hunt, kill, and eat a number of aquatic species.

What Jaguars Eat

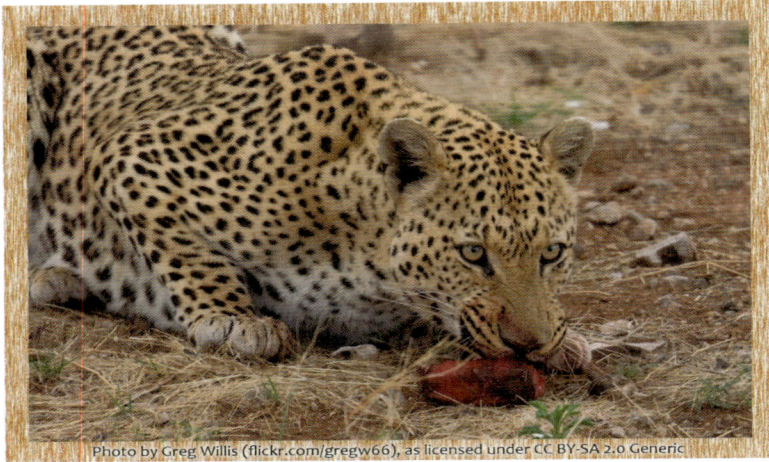

Photo by Greg Willis (flickr.com/gregw66), as licensed under CC BY-SA 2.0 Generic

Jaguars are not picky about their food. They eat any of 85 different species! Their most common meals include wild pigs called peccaries, tapirs, the largest rodents called capybara, armadillos, and deer. They also eat turtles and caimans, reptiles that are closely related to crocodiles and alligators!

Hunting

The name jaguar comes from the native word 'yaguar', which means 'he that kills with one leap'. Ambush, this is how the jaguar hunts. Although they are fast runners, jaguars don't usually chase their prey. They stalk their prey and pounce at the perfect moment. They deliver a crushing bite to the skull and their prey is dead.

Bite

Photo by William Warby (flickr.com/wwarby), as licensed under CC BY 2.0 Generic

Jaguars have an incredibly powerful bite, strong enough to crush the skulls of their prey. Their strong bite is what allows them to penetrate the hard skin of caimans and shells of turtles. Some scientists say that the jaguar has the 4th most powerful bite in the animal kingdom, behind only American alligators and 2 species of crocodile!

Senses

Photo by Rennett Stowe (flickr.com/tomsaint), as licensed under CC BY 2.0 Generic

Like all cats, jaguars can see in the dark. Their eyesight is very good and they can hunt easily even in the darkness. Their sense of hearing is also good. But their sense of smell isn't quite as good other cats. So they don't really use their nose to hunt, they use their eyes and ears.

Behavior

Photo by Charlie Marshall (flickr.com/100915417@N07), as licensed under CC BY 2.0 Generic

Most jaguars are active during dusk and dawn. However, in some places they are also active during daytime. Jaguars are solitary animals, they don't live in groups, they live and hunt alone. The only time jaguars are seen together is to mate and when a mother is bringing up her young.

Territory

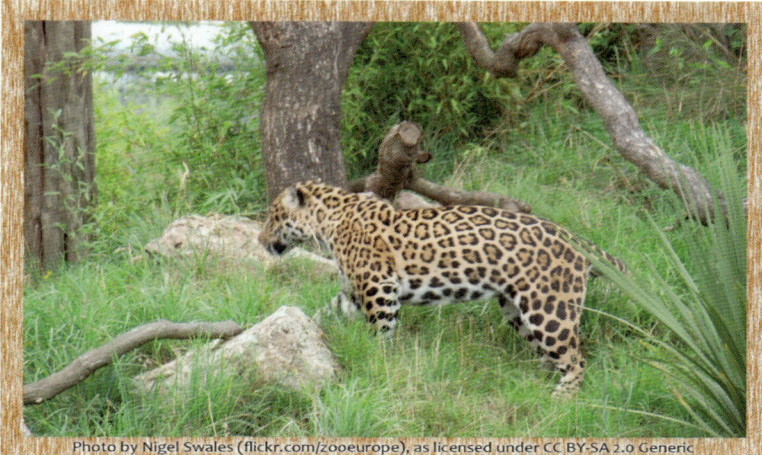

Photo by Nigel Swales (flickr.com/zooeurope), as licensed under CC BY-SA 2.0 Generic

Jaguars are territorial animals. Each jaguar has their own territory. They urinate and scratch trees with their claws on the border of their territory to tell other jaguars to keep out. The territories of male jaguars are larger than females, and male territories often encompass several female territories.

Sounds

Photo by Eric Kilby (flickr.com/ekilby), as licensed under CC BY-SA 2.0 Generic

Jaguars, like the 3 other big cats, can roar. Other cats can't roar, only the big cats can. Jaguars roar to warn others they're entering its territory, to attract a mate, and to express anger. Jaguars also make several different sounds including grunts and meows.

Breeding

Jaguars have no breeding season and can mate any time of the year. The only time adult jaguars are seen together is to mate. Female jaguars are pregnant for around 100 days.

Baby Jaguar

Photo by Nick Jewell (flickr.com/macjewell), as licensed under CC BY 2.0 Generic

Female jaguars give birth to 1-4 cubs. When they are newborn, baby jaguars are blind and helpless. Their mother protects them fiercely, even from their own father.

Life of a Jaguar

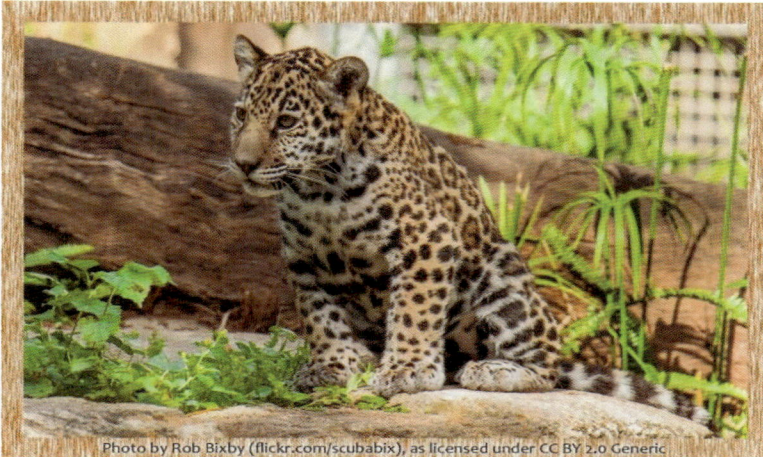

Photo by Rob Bixby (flickr.com/scubabix), as licensed under CC BY 2.0 Generic

Mother jaguars will feed and protect her young until they reach one year old. At that time, the young will start learning to hunt, but they still stay with their mother. Jaguars leave their mother at about 2 years old to find their own territory. They reach maturity when they reach 2-4 years old. In the wild, a jaguar's lifespan is only about 11-12 years. But in captivity they can live up to 20 years.

Humans and Jaguars

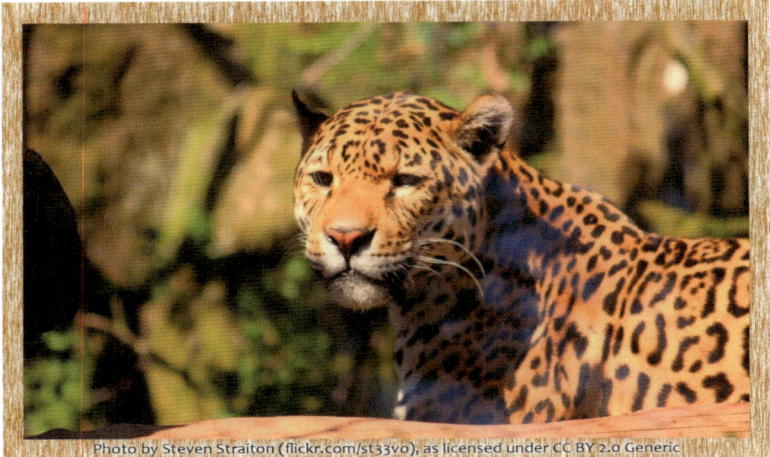

Photo by Steven Straiton (flickr.com/st33vo), as licensed under CC BY 2.0 Generic

Being the only big cat in the Americas, it's no surprise that jaguars have many, many ancient stories about them. There are lots of jaguar depictions in ancient ruins. Today, jaguars are often seen as a symbol of royalty, strength, and beauty.

Near Threatened

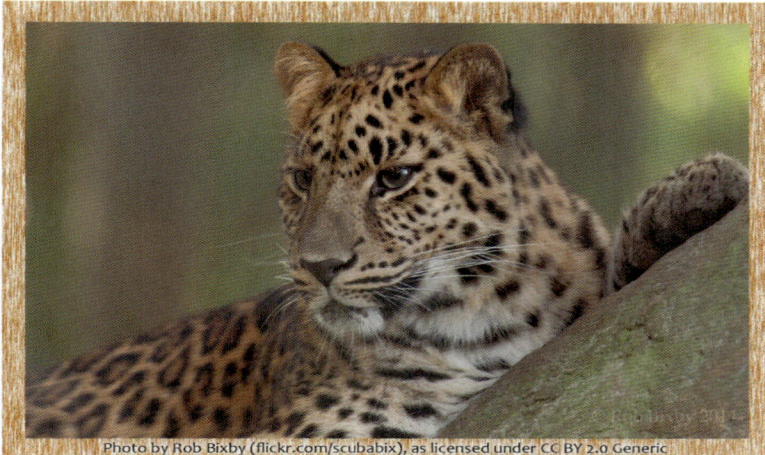

Photo by Rob Bixby (flickr.com/scubabix), as licensed under CC BY 2.0 Generic

However, not everybody sees the jaguar as a beautiful animal. They are considered to be pests by some people for killing their cattle. Jaguars are sometimes shot for this, and also for their fur. They used to be heavily hunted for their fur. Today, most countries have laws to protect the jaguar. Jaguars are not an endangered species; they are listed as a Near Threatened species, but their population is decreasing as their natural habitat gets destroyed.

Relatives

Photo by BurellierC (flickr.com/101425717@N06), as licensed under CC BY 2.0 Generic

Jaguars are part of the panthera genus, also known as the big cats. Their closest relatives are lions, tigers, leopards, and snow leopards. They are also related to all other cats such as bobcats, cheetahs, cougars, and even house cats.

Black Panther

Photo by Bernard DUPONT (flickr.com/berniedup), as licensed under CC BY-SA 2.0 Generic

Most jaguars have yellow fur with black spots, but some jaguars have black fur. Such jaguars are called 'black panthers'. But what exactly is a black panther? Black panthers are not a separate species. A black panther is simply a panther (a big cat) that is colored black. There are also black leopards, and sometimes even black tigers, these are all called black panthers.

Get the next book in this series!

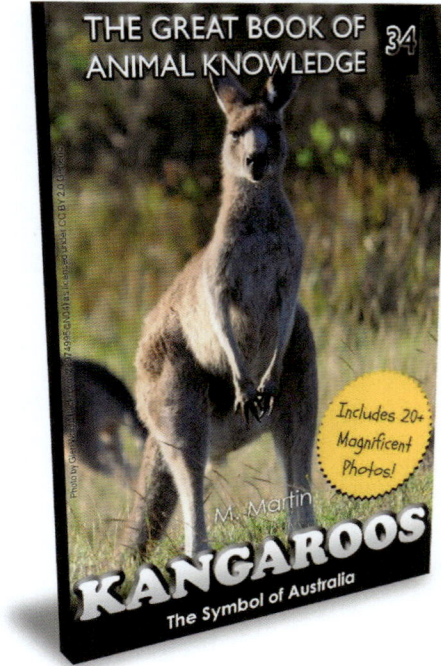

KANGAROO: The Symbol of Australia

Log on to Facebook.com/GazelleCB for more info

Tip: Use the key-phrase "The Great Book of Animal Knowledge" when searching for books in this series.

GAZELLE
CHILDREN'S BOOKS

For more information about our
books, discounts and updates,
please Like us on FaceBook!

Facebook.com/GazelleCB

Printed in Great Britain
by Amazon